#MOMLIFE INC

7 Essential Lessons for Building a
Million-Dollar Start-Up as a Busy Mom

LEAH CUPPS

None of this would be possible without my extraordinary husband David Cupps. Thank you for everything. I love you!

CONTENTS

PREFACE   IX

INTRODUCTION   1
HELLO FELLOW MOMMY!
Who is the Mom behind Momlife, Inc.?

CHAPTER ONE   22
WRITE THE VISION
Developing the Dream: Tips for Writing Your Vision

CHAPTER TWO   36
WORK SMARTER, NOT HARDER
Applying the Principles of Parkinson's Law

CHAPTER THREE   52
JUMP FIRST, ASK QUESTIONS LATER
Fighting the Fear in Perfectionism

CHAPTER FOUR   68

INVEST IN YOUR EDUCATION
Making the Investment in Yourself

CHAPTER FIVE   80

DELEGATE THE MUNDANE
Getting Out of Your Own Way

CHAPTER SIX   92

FIND YOUR PURPOSE
Choosing Purpose over Passion

CHAPTER SEVEN   102

DEVELOPING GRIT
Discover the Skill of Perserverence

CONCLUSION   113

FINAL WORDS

RESOURCES   116

Every journey begins with a single step

MAYA ANGELOU

Hello friend! First, I want to thank you for grabbing my book! It's a big world and I'm just a small-town girl from Indiana, but I've accomplished something incredible and I know you can too. That's why I wrote this book.

As multitasking mommies, our dreams sometimes get put on the back burner when we struggle to keep up with the daily demands of motherhood—running a household and, for some of us, running a business. If you grabbed this book, then I'm guessing you have a great idea or have already started a business that you are passionate about. You are likely looking from some inspiration or even a little help to take things to the next level. Am I right?

In the following pages, I'm going to share with

you my story—how I, alongside my husband, built a multi-million-dollar company by working less than 30 hours a week, and how we did it in just 18 months. I'll detail how I did it all while having a 1-year-old daughter at home, and how I continued my upward mobility even after becoming pregnant with and delivering my son. (Raise your hand if you've ever breastfed a baby at your desk. Thank you, Boppy!) As I share my experiences and lessons with you, I'm also going to challenge you to level up your own dreams as well.

HOW TO USE THIS BOOK:

I want you to use this book however suits your needs best. Read it back-to-front or front-to-back. If it makes more sense, jump to the chapters that inspire you most.

All I ask is that you complete the challenges I've created. There are pre-set challenges at the end of each chapter, placed there to not only inspire you to act, but also to help you shift your ideas about what is possible. So, let's get started and have some fun!

WHO IS THE MOM BEHIND MOMLIFE, INC.?

Imagine sitting and having a rare quiet moment. Maybe you're free from work or the kids are taking a nap. In that moment you think, "Is this all that life has to offer? Could there be something more?" I believe this is where most entrepreneurs start.

We sometimes discover a feeling deep down in our spirit—one that whispers in our ear the promise of a greater purpose for our lives. I've experienced that feeling twice in my life. The first time was when I left my corporate job to become a freelance graphic designer, and the second time was shortly after I had my first child. But, the real story begins when I met my soul mate, David.

I had been struggling along as a freelance

designer for about 4 years when I met this hunk of a man I now get to call my husband. We instantly bonded over things like sprint triathlons, growing up on rural Indiana farms, and being part of the world of entrepreneurship. We both had a lot of ideas about businesses we'd like to start, but we always made excuses for ourselves on why it wasn't the right time. However, by combining our skills and our financial resources, it suddenly felt like anything was possible.

In year one of our marriage, we launched our first business—a photo booth rental company. Our motivation for that business was clear: we had both come into the marriage with debt, and this business would be the income source to pay it off.

During the weekdays, we both worked hard. David toiled as a medical sales director and I kept it up as a freelance designer. On the weekends, we ran events, schlepping around a 70-pound photo booth to weddings, bar/

bat mitzvahs, and other events across central Indiana. We used the extra income to pay off all our debts (except for our home). The first couple of years were exciting and fun, but after realizing that we had no social life and never saw our friends anymore, the excitement started to wane. Meanwhile, I became pregnant and was about to have our first baby. That added to our desire to spend the weekends at home with our growing family.

Our daughter, Savannah, soon entered the world, and like for many parents, our lives forever changed. What surprised me the most about becoming a mother was that I still craved having a business. More than just being a mother, I desired a creative outlet for all the ideas and dreams I had before she came. Those entrepreneurial desires and dreams may have changed a tad, but they certainly still existed.

Juggling a baby and my freelance projects had its challenges, but I was steadfast at making it work. Still, in the back of our minds, David and I felt like we could accomplish so much more. We both dreamed of having a product to sell online, providing enough income for a comfortable lifestyle while allowing us to leverage our time more efficiently. However, we both had a preconceived notion of how all that would look.

Maybe it was because of our newfound "Shark Tank" addiction, but we mistakenly believed that we had to invent something to have a physical products business. We were stuck on the idea that if we had a product then it had to be a ground-breaking brainchild to be successful. I'm happy to say that we learned you don't have to be a great inventor to create a successful business.

In the summer of 2014, I was still doing my freelance graphic design business and David was working in outside sales. One afternoon, I met with a client who had a line of natural, homemade beauty products. My 1-year-old daughter, Savannah, tagged along for the meeting and flicked cheerios on the floor while talked about her need for a new logo and attractive packaging.

At one point in the conversation, I said "You should sell your products on Amazon." She replied that it was very difficult to sell products there. I agreed, although I didn't really know much about selling products on Amazon. I knew that Amazon was a huge platform and that I was an Amazon Prime devotee (can you say diaper delivery?). As I drove home, I thought to myself, "Why don't I sell products on Amazon and take my own advice?"

So, when I got home I Googled "How to sell products on Amazon." That moment literally changed our lives forever. I discovered a course called "Amazing Selling Machine" which taught the steps on how to privately label and sell products through the Amazon platform.

We did not have to reinvent the wheel; we simply had to create our own brand. Hello, game changer!

David and I became obsessed with launching our own line of branded products. After a couple of days of researching products, we decided to launch seaweed powder. It doesn't sound too sexy, but Dr. Oz had just done a segment on the benefits of seaweed powder wraps at home, and the products were selling successfully online. I got to work on a logo and packaging while David sourced some jars and found a place we could order in bulk.

Our first production run was anything but glamorous. David and I would spend late nights side by side, measuring and filling jars of seaweed, hand-applying labels and shrink-wrapping them with a heat gun until our fingertips were burning. Within a few weeks, we were finally ready to launch our first product.

The product launched and it was moderately

successful. That gave us the proof that we were onto something, and it also gave us the courage to expand our line of products. David had amazing faith in our idea, so over the next 18 months he invested every one of his work bonuses into our company. To this day, we have never taken out a bank loan or had to borrow money.

As we added more products and expanded into the new categories, the business grew quickly. David and I felt that we had finally found our sweet spot and began to taste success. I loved designing and creating products, and creating brands was a blast as well. David was great at negotiating with suppliers and optimizing our Amazon listings. Although David helped with the business as much as he could, he was becoming increasingly successful at his own job. Eventually, it required him to be away for 2-3 nights a week.

In 2015, we become pregnant with our second child. That news, coupled with the long days on the road and the nights away from home, made David realize that it was time to make an exit from his job. We were still reinvesting the profits from our company back into the business, so striking out completely on our own was a huge leap of faith. I was on a mission, and we lovingly called it "Operation: Bring Daddy Home." I was determined to create so much opportunity with our business that David would have to quit his job by the end of 2016 and join our little company full time. During this time, our monthly sales soared, from $100,00 per month to over $250,000 per month. We started paying ourselves salary that could support our entire family.

Our second baby, Lincoln, came in March 2016, and to our surprise, David was able leave his job by July 1st. Shortly after David left his job, he caught wind that some companies that sold physical products with a storefront on Amazon were selling for 2-3 times their EBITA (earnings before interest, taxes, and amortization). We had always had the idea of selling our company eventually, but hearing that news made it somehow more attainable. By December of 2016, we had put the entire company up for sale. The offers came in quickly and we accepted an offer for more than we had ever imagined. Of course, like many things we had worked for, it did not go as planned.

It took 6 months and several lawyers haggling over the details of the Asset Purchase Agreement before we were finally able to close on the business. That was yet another dream fulfilled for us. It opened even more possibilities for our family's future and inspired this book.

. . . .

Now, I'm sure you are thinking, "Okay, that's a nice story, but why should I care? Why should I bother reading this book? There's no way I could do the same thing. What's so special about me?" Well, I can tell you there is nothing so special about me and that fact is exciting.

Why? Because it means that the anyone can achieve the level of success that I have by applying the same principles that I applied to my life, and by coupling that with the right opportunities. Three years ago, I was making less than $100,000 a year and then 3 years later I ended up selling my company for several million dollars. Along the way, I discovered 7 principles that powered my unusual success.

I would love to see my readers apply these 7 principles to their everyday life. At the end of each chapter, I've provided some "chapter challenges" designed to give you some tactical applications for these successful principles I learned. My dream is to help you have the life you have always imagined. I'm here to tell you yes, it is possible and I am excited to get you there by sharing the lessons I learned.

Big ideas
have small
beginnings

#MOMLIFEINC

WRITE THE VISION

CHAPTER ONE

"Write the vision; make it plain."

- Habakkuk 2:2

....

It was the fall of 2012 as I stood in the kitchen of my beautiful new home overlooking a small lake in Indiana. Two glasses of wine sat on the kitchen island while my husband and I chatted away about the happenings of the day. Suddenly, I pushed up on my tiptoes and told David to wait for one second while I ran into the other room. When I returned I was holding my laptop open, fingers poised on the screen. "I want you to hear this," I said excitedly. The words I read aloud perfectly described our current situation.

I was standing in a front of the man of my dreams, in a home that was very different from my cape cod fixer upper in downtown Indianapolis. While tears welled up in my eyes, I described our neighborhood and the BMW I was driving. I detailed how I was now parking in our attached garage to carry groceries inside. My previous home had a detached garage, so I had to haul hefty grocery bags through the rain and into my back door which was no fun at all. My husband looked at me with intrigue, and he patiently listened as I regaled him with every minute detail of our current circumstances. I kept getting more and more excited, and finally when my tirade was finished I slapped the laptop closed and I said, "I wrote this a year ago before we even met." Like some paranormal soothsayer, I had predicted our exact future down to the granite counter tops and white baseboard trim.

I wrote down these details of my future life in the hopes that all my dreams would someday come true. With a little bit of boldness in my heart I closed my eyes and wrote down my dreamy scenario as if it had already happened. I went as far as to describe the smells, textures, and feelings associated with being in that exact kitchen. I wrote about this amazing man in my life too. I also jotted down what I wanted to happen, as if I were simply recalling the day while it played out. I called this exercise "creating a future vision." The main idea was to write my future as if it were happening presently. I was mentally acting out my dreams and reporting the results a year in advance.

From doing this, I learned how incredibly powerful it is to have a vision and write it down. I discovered how, if you project your vision (say it, write it down on paper, etc.) you put into motion a powerful subconscious transformation. It's almost like a trick of the mind, making it believe that these things had already happened and therefore will re-happen. This is just one way to create a vision for yourself and make it come true. I have mimicked this approach in several different ways, but writing down a "future vision" seemed to be the most powerful.

Let's take a step back here. What if I had not written about meeting the man of my dreams or finding our perfectly decorated home together? What if it all was just something I had only hoped for, and I simply mentioned it to myself in passing but never really sent out the message to the universe? It comes down to this: If you keep doing what you've always done, you will keep getting what you've always got.

So, I believe that, many times, we get caught up in the day-to-day grind and we forget about chasing our dreams and goals. We stop wanting something better for ourselves because we either believe it doesn't exist or we think it's too far out of our reach. Even more common, we believe that we don't deserve a better future.

We forget how powerful our mind-set is, and we neglect to believe that we can create our vision with faith and conviction to achieve our ambitions. If we don't, we fail to ever live out our dreams. So, this exercise is something I do often – once every year or so. Sometimes I wait until everything in my 'future vision' comes true before I write another one. Sometimes I don't.

Having a vision means refraining from setting limits on what you can accomplish. I'll be honest and say that when I described my ideal husband in my little essay, there was a small part of me that didn't believe a man like him even existed. There was a slightly larger part of me that didn't believe I deserved a suave, smart, and sexy dude. Even though I hesitated to believe he existed on a conscious level, I still wrote his subconscious existence into being in a concrete way - almost as if I forced myself into believing he was real and waiting on me.

No matter how outlandish your dreams seem, you still need to know where you are going. It's the only way to enjoy the fruits of your labor.

FOR ME, THE TOP THREE BENEFITS OF "FUTURE VISION WRITING" ARE AS FOLLOWS:

1. *It creates motivation to power through obstacles.*

2. *It allows you to align your everyday action with your goals.*

3. *It inspires and propels you to move towards your dreams.*

Put simply, you must have a vision. We all need a road map that leads us to our ideal destination, but unfortunately, Siri won't do the trick.

YOUR FUTURE VISION: THE SCIENCE BEHIND IT

Be diligent and don't take my word for any of it. The benefits of constructing a future vision are something scientists have been studying for years. In fact, an article published by neurologists at Wellcome Trust Centre for Neuroimaging at the Institute of Neurology in London have discovered substantial research which supports the idea that creating a futuristic vision in your mind can improve the odds of that vision coming true. In their published study, the scientists wrote, "The ability to construct a hypothetical scenario in one's imagination prior to it actually occurring may afford greater accuracy in predicting its eventual outcome."

Think of it this way: Our minds are really just a cognitive construction zone. When we access our memories, we are simply re-constructing past experiences and filling in the gaps with our imagination. In the same way, when we envision our future we are using our imagination to construct a new outcome. In that way, it's critical to use our inherent construction equipment to actively create a desirable lifestyle. The findings in this study continue on to say that being able to accurately and richly enact possible future states before making a decision would help to evaluate the desirability of different outcomes, and it also assists the planning processes needed to make those outcomes happen. So, even from a scientific prospective, it's clear that we need to plan for a better future.

CHAPTER CHALLENGE

Take out something to write with and find a quiet space with no distractions. My favorite time to do things like this is during my kid's nap time – am I right, moms? Take a deep, cleansing breath (or three) before you begin, trying to exhale away all the distractions of your day. Once you feel centered and cleared-headed, write about what your perfect life would look like a year from now. When you describe this day, be sure to put some real emotion behind it.

Note how it feels to have the people and things you want in your life. Maybe, like me, you picture yourself freshly showered after a killer workout, sitting across from your amazing husband, enjoying a glass of wine while you talk about how unbelievably successful your 1 year-old business has become. Maybe yours will be a bit different, and that's ok. The point is, as you write, to include as many details as possible, painting a verbal picture of what it's like to be there in that moment. Maybe touch base on the smell of your man's cologne, or perhaps concentrate on the taste of drinking an expensive pinot noir at your favorite restaurant. The idea is simple: Plot out that perfect day so that you can convince your mind that it's already happening, and make sure you capture your biggest goals achieved in the process.

It may seem a little "new-agey" at first, but trust me when I say that nothing is more practical than having an inspirational and ambitious vision/goal for yourself. I write one or more every year, and then I tuck it away until a later date. Sometimes, when I am feeling discouraged or directionless, I will pull it out and read it to remind myself that I have something great waiting for me in the future if I can just get through the necessary steps of today.

In my opinion, writing down your vision is the fun part. Looking back at it is incredibly rewarding too. So, go ahead and have some fun with your future. Grab your writing weapon of choice and start jotting down your unique vision right now. It's okay; I'll wait.

A woman
without a vision
for her future,
always returns
to her past

WORK SMARTER, NOT HARDER

"Work expands so as to fill the time available for its completion."

- Cyril Northcote Parkinson

I had three hours a day. Three precious hours a day was all I had to clobber a huge list of to-dos' as CEO (and everything else) in our little start-up company. My husband was working daunting hours and traveling on the road to fund the growth of our business, and I was given the task to push our little venture forward and complete, "Operation: Bring Daddy Home". Meanwhile, I only had the three hours in the morning when my daughter attended preschool to focus on what needed to be done.

For a year of my life, those three hours a day were all I had to achieve the seemingly impossible, and yet I pulled it off. I took our company sales from $100,000 to $250,000 a month, three hours (and a few nights) at the time. Ten years ago, I'm certain that three hours a day wouldn't be enough time for anything, especially scaling a business of this magnitude. But, by leveraging the FBA program (Fulfillment By Amazon) and by utilizing virtual assistants (more on that in a later chapter), I made three hours a day work. Having a set time to work each day pushed me to focus my efforts on only the important projects. About halfway through this stage, I discovered that my method had a name: Parkinson's Law. Parkinson's Law states: "Work expands so as to fill the time available for its completion." Sounds interesting, right? Let's take a closer look.

In 1955, Cyril Northcote Parkinson, a famous British historian and author, wrote a book called "Parkinson's Law: The Pursuit of Progress." He discovered that if you are given a week to complete a 2-hour task, the task will become more complex and time consuming to the fill the time allotted. On the other hand, he surmised that if you are only given those two precious hours to accomplish something, it will miraculously get done. Unfortunately, our culture seems to believe that working harder and longer is somehow more effective than working smarter and faster, but Parkinson's Law proves that that's simply not the case.

Putting in long hours and boasting a 60-hour work week seems to garner more respect than only working 15 hours in a week, even though doing so is the American Dream. In fact, I would go as far as to say that most people, when they hear about such things, believe the worker must have done a sloppy job, or that the job must have been super easy. Stepping back to look at the activities that fill up your day might allow you to cut an average 8-hour work day in half. Do you ever sit at your desk and just let your mind wander? How much time do you spend scrolling through Facebook or sorting unimportant email? That precious time could be better spent, and thus it could be applied to the bigger picture – Parkinson's Law.

Another lesser known principle, also proposed by Parkinson, was his "Law of Triviality," also known "bikeshedding." Parkinson's Law of Triviality observes that humans tend to devote large amounts of time to unimportant details while the more important matters go unattended. The term "bikeshedding" came about during one of his many laboratory observations. Parkinson observed a committee of people who were in charge of approving plans for a nuclear plant. As the process unfolded, he noticed that a disproportionate amount of attention was given to the design of a bike shed, a relatively unimportant detail. This limited the committee's time to focus on more important details, like the actual design and function of the plant. If only Parkinson had seen me planning a birthday party for my daughter!

Do all those minute details like glitter stickers on the invitations matter? Isn't it more important that the kids just have fun, rather than every detail of the princess theme being carried through from beginning to end? (Darn you, Pinterest!) I think this principle can be applied to so many aspects of our daily lives, both personally and in business. We have to take those moments where we step back and say, "Wait. Should this be a priority?"

APPLYING THE PRINCIPLES OF PARKINSON'S LAW

In my case, I had to stay on task because there was a very tangible time limit to my work day. I couldn't ever let my mind stray from the dedicated list of tasks I had planned for the day because my time constraints wouldn't allow it. In other words, having a finite amount of time to work on my goals created a sense of urgency. That urgency then propelled me forward through my long list of to-dos'. Never assume that having just a few hours a day to work will be less effective than having a full eight. Sometimes less is more. You can make it as big or be as successful as someone working long hours, because Parkinson's Law states that having a finite amount of time can make people more productive due to the fact that it forces the focus on what's most important. So, don't fall victim to the self-perpetuated lie that you don't have enough time to get something done. Parkinson's Law has clarified the possibilities: Sometimes, you can get a lot more done with a lot less time. Now let's talk about what that looks like.

How do I bust through the never-ending laundry, dishes, and entrepreneurial duties with just a few hours to spare? On any given day, I have a long list of items that need my immediate attention. Here are the methods I use to get it all done:

1. HAVE A CUP OF COFFEE. ....

I know what you're thinking. Really? I bought this book so you could tell me to drink a cup of coffee? Well, it may surprise you that even though over 85% of the U.S. population drinks coffee, very few are "coffee literate" or well educated on the brain-boosting benefits of java. Fewer still know about coffee's ability to = increase productivity.

You see, when caffeine hits the brain it suppresses a neurotransmitter called adenosine. Adenosine is what affects your attention span, your alertness, and your sleeping patterns. When you wake in the morning, your level of adenosine is very low, but as you go throughout your day, the levels of adenosine rise and consequently, your attention span and alertness rise along with it. Now, wouldn't it be awesome if there were a way to shortcut this process and put a little extra pep in your step in your morning? Cue the cup of joe!

Studies have also shown that caffeine can help boost your learning curve by as much as 10%. And as mothers trying to solve problems (like, why are pack and plays so hard to set up?) and as career warriors trying to continuously solve problems with our business, we are on a constant learning curve. With all the amazing benefits of coffee, it's clear to see why I recommend it as the first step to an incredibly productive day.

2. MAKE A LIST

I have a mantra—if it doesn't make my task list, it doesn't happen. I have always been a list girl, but when I began juggling business and parenting, it become a mainstay in my survival kit. I keep a special notebook that I use just for making my daily lists. There are many benefits to keeping a daily task list.

First of all, they give the list-maker the capacity to select and prioritize what needs done. By writing down daily tasks, you can see the bigger picture form and can choose what you would like to work on first. Lists help you form a path and a plan for the day, week, or month. Instead of sitting at your desk for 15 minutes deciding where to start, you can just scan your daily list of to-dos' and pick your first accomplishment for the day.

Lists can help you avoid anxiety as well. There is nothing worse than feeling overwhelmed by having so many things to do, but if you have a clear list of tasks to tackle, you have a greater sense of control. On my list, I try to number and capture each item that needs done for the day (or over several days). If I complete a task, I put a big, fat satisfactory line through that item. If I don't complete that task for the day I move it to the next day's list of duties. It's as simple as that, and it's not a difficult habit to form.

If you've never been a list girl, I can't tell you the satisfaction of crossing out the task at hand and moving on to the next item. But some days, I just have trouble getting the engines firing (usually the mornings after my daughter crawls into my bed at 3am). One approach that helps me to kick off a productive day is to start with the easiest, quickest task on my list. Maybe it's adding an email address for a new employee or doing a quick Facebook post on our business page. Either way, it's something that takes less than 15 minutes and it then becomes my first achievement of the day, which motivates me to do more.

To understand why this is so important, we must take a look at the science of motivation. Motivation happens when your dopamine (the feel good chemical in your brain) spikes in the anticipation of something good happening or about to happen. You can actually train your brain to feed off small bursts of dopamine simply by creating a series of rewarding experiences.

What is a small rewarding experience? You guessed it: Crossing off that first item on your to-do list. So, if we can knock out a few easy, quick tasks at the start off our day, we can then increase our motivation to continue on and complete more tasks successfully.

4. JUST TOUCH IT

On the flip side, if an item has been on my list for several days, it starts to annoy me. In turn, it creates a sense of urgency (and dread) to get it done. So, another tactic I employ is to "just touch it." if I can just take one or two steps toward finishing a larger project, I am more likely to complete it. As the saying goes: "To eat a big sandwich, you have to take one bite at a time."

As an example, let's say I have a big product photo shoot coming up. This involves scheduling a photographer, renting a studio, coordinating models, finding props and securing child care. But, if I am feeling overwhelmed, I tend to break down that bigger project into smaller, more digestible bites. Step one: schedule the photographer. I can cross that off my list for the day and move on to the next task instead of staring blankly out the window, feeling overwhelmed and numb by the sheer weight of the entire undertaking.

5. LIGHTS, COFFEE, ACTION!

Most importantly it's important to simply create action. If we start out by creating a vision for our business and then we see a favorable future, we always have a way to take action. Whether it's as small as sending out a few emails to suppliers, or finally purchasing that domain name for a business idea we have, a vision combined with an action we take towards that goal (large or small) thereby creates an unstoppable momentum that we can build on each day.

For me, not every day is home run of accomplishments, but I always take some sort of action to move towards my goal regardless. Even the smallest of actions keep my confidence boosted and my mind on target. If I am taking action, I feel like, "Okay, maybe this is possible and I can pull it off." Small actions have a way of adding up over time, and we all need a foundation to build our dreams upon.

Even on the days when I am not exactly crushing my to-do list, I may just have another cup of coffee and read a great non-fiction book to regroup and reprioritize. Even that type of action helps me to stay motivated and feel refueled, so don't feel bad if you have to do that from time to time as well.

You are a productive genius. You just don't know it yet! As mothers, we are already master multi-taskers, constantly juggling all types of family priorities, and solving all kinds of problems.

I truly believe that, if you are able to carve out just a few focused hours a day, you can power through what it would take most office workers a week to complete.

It's time to challenge yourself to achieve what you thought was possible. Here's how:

1. Make a list of at least 3 items that you have on your to-do list. (Preferably, something that inches you closer to your goals). An example could be having a logo created for your business or finding a supplier your new product idea.

2. Next to each item, write down the number of hours you think it would take to give that task your full and best attention until it's complete. Ball park figures are just fine.

3. Now in the third column, CUT THAT TIME IN HALF. If you thought it would take you a week, then give yourself three days. If you think it will take two hours, give yourself one.

4. Finally, you are off to the races! Go complete the task, and in the very last column write down how many hours it actually took you to complete the task.

In all the excitement, don't forget to reflect on how good it feels to check it off your list. Give yourself props for how you crushed your preconceived notions regarding how long it would take you. Sometimes, it's okay to gloat.

JUMP FIRST ASK QUESTIONS LATER

CHAPTER THREE

> "Only in the leap from the lion's head
> will he prove his worth."
> *- Indiana Jones*

I will never forget the stench of the fresh seaweed powder that wafted up into the air of the apartment we rented for 3 months while our house was being built. We were bottling our own line of beauty products to sell on Amazon. com, and consequently, our place smelled like a fish cannery. Wait a minute; I'm getting ahead of myself here. Let's back up a few steps.

After settling on the idea of selling products on Amazon, I quickly shared it with David and he was dazzled by the idea. We quickly went to work researching (aka "Googling") anything we could find on private labeled products being sold on the platform. It didn't take long before we stumbled across an entire batch of YouTube videos boasting huge sales numbers from Amazon private label products. For a few weeks, it was a back and forth banter consisting of "Did you see this video on sourcing products?" or "Have you seen this guy that launched his product in just 2 weeks?" The concept of Amazon private label was fairly fresh at the time, and for us, it was the opportunity that we had been waiting for.

I quickly leapt into action. Product choice? Check. Name and logo? Check. Label? Check. David found a supplier, the packaging, and handed over his bank card. Check, check, and check. You get the idea. Within a couple of weeks, we had huge bags of seaweed powder, large boxes of jars, and several yards of labels being delivered to the hallway of our apartment building. Thankfully, my daughter was sleeping 12 hours a night at the time (thank you, Babywise) and we seized the opportunity while it was hot.

David and I spent most nights staying up late, scooping powder into an small jar that sat on the kitchen scale. When that was done, we had to seal each jar by hand with a heat gun. It wasn't easy, but we made it work. Just a few weeks later our product went live on Amazon and began garnering sales. We were in business.

This story is near and dear to me, so I share it with you for a reason. Notice how we didn't waste time waffling over what product we would sell. See how we didn't stall by trying to find the perfect product or business name. We just jumped in with our guns blazing. We simply took a leap of faith on a new venture and it paid off big time. This approach to leap first and ask questions later – letting the cards fall the way they may while we focus on our future vision - has been the most profound catalyst for our success.

My experience leads me to believe that many people get stuck in a rut because they are trying to find the perfect product, the perfect company name, the perfect time to work, or the perfect opportunity to start. I often think that, deep down, people are afraid to start a business, and so, hiding behind an excuse like, "Well, it wasn't the right time or the right product" is an easy way to avoid failure. In my opinion, the best way to grow and learn in the business world is to throw your ideas on the wall and see if they stick. If you are waiting for a knock on the door, some divine intervention, or a guarantee that your business is going to be "the end of all business successes," you're going to be left empty handed, that's for sure.

FIGHTING THE FEAR IN PERFECTIONISM

I have heard it said that perfectionism is a form of fear, and I whole-heartedly agree. If you wait for everything to be perfect, then you may never reach any of your goals – even the small ones. Take a leap of faith by just taking the first step. If you make a mistake, simply fix it. Try to learn from it as best you can, but don't let that be the reason you give up trying.

Here's the thing ladies, you have a gift! Something inside of you is unique, and that's means you are uniquely qualified to share that gift with the world.

If you slave away at making something "perfect," you may not be able express your true purpose. The value your life possesses may not be recognized because it's being hidden behind your futile attempts to be flawless. To get over your perfectionist fears and start taking a leap of faith, I suggest the following habits:

1. TAKE A SMALL LEAP OF FAITH

Don't let fear stop you or self-doubt creep into your head. Take a small leap of faith toward your dream, and do it often. Maybe that will be just simply securing your Tax ID number to start your business or grabbing a website domain for the venture idea you have. These small steps of faith, a.k.a. believing in your dream despite adversity, will give you the confidence to move onto the next step. . . and the next.

2. PLAY OUT THE WORST CASE SCENARIO

When looking at starting a new business or taking any step of faith in life, it's common for all kinds of fears and objections to well up inside of us. But, I like to take the worst case scenario and let that play out in words with my husband. We will discuss it, accept that it can happen, and just keep moving forward.

For example, let's say that you want to start an online business selling baby clothes. To get started you need to invest your time and a few hundred dollars setting up a website and a getting few products to stock your store. Or, maybe you test the idea by selling on Etsy. Either way, what do you lose if the business fails? Well, you lose a few hundred dollars and a few weeks of your time. It doesn't feel so awful, right!? Now what if you become successful and are able to grow your business? The upsides to that are unlimited. So, in most cases, it behooves you to take action and to risk the time and cost of failure in order to try and live out your dreams.

THINK ABOUT THIS:

Will this "failure" matter in 5 years? Or will you still be talking about that business that you always wanted to start 5 years ago?

3. LIVE WITH FAILURE AND LEARN FROM MISTAKES

On the contrary, failure, in many cases, can ultimately lead us to the business we were always meant for. In our case, the first business we started was in the natural, organic beauty space. The business did well, but we discovered we did not have the passion for it like we did for baby products. So, while that business was not the most successful venture for us, it taught us how to design and create products to sell online, which ultimately led us to the larger, more successful business we were meant to run.

4. DON'T HIDE BEHIND PERFECTION, OR MAKE EXCUSES FOR YOURSELF.

Many times, we hide behind our idea of something needs to be perfect before we present it to the world. My approach is just the opposite. I like to get an idea in front of as many people as possible so I can get feedback, refine the concept, then make improvements. The feedback people give on various products often surprises me. My insecurities often get shut down by positive feedback I wasn't expecting. So, don't wait for the perfect idea or the perfect product; get started and get something out there now so you can start getting feedback. Ultimately, that's the first step towards getting you to the dream of running your own successful business.

REALIZATION

If it weren't for my willingness to take risks and put a product out there before it was perfect, I am certain that I would not be where I am today, vision or not. Taking a leap of faith is more than just the leap itself; it's telling the world that you believe in yourself and not being afraid of possible hiccups or failures. It says, "I am creating something that matters," and therefore, it makes you matter.

Because of those reasons, many people feel as though they don't have anything valuable to offer or that they don't deserve success. Most often, it's moms who have fallen victim to the "I'm just a mom" mentality. I am here to tell you that you do have something valuable to offer, and though it may be hidden at this moment, it's certainly worth sharing with the world. You've just got to get out there and take the first step.

Creativity is what happens when the rules run out. So, this 3-step challenge is designed to be a simple solution to help you get started:

1. Write down 3 items you've had on your business to do list.
   Examples can be reaching out to your ideal business influencer – someone you've been wanting to become a partner with to display your products. Or perhaps, make the investment in a website domain reserved while you start sourcing products.

2. DO NOT take no for an answer; where there is a will, there is a way.

3. Give yourself 24 hours to complete the three items on your to-do list.

Do these challenges to the best of your ability. That way, if you begin at 10 a.m. on Monday morning, you can expect a smile on your face and three check marks on your to-do list by Tuesday morning.

Strive for progress, not perfection

#MOMLIFEINC

INVEST IN YOUR EDUCATION

CHAPTER FOUR

"Do the best you can until you know better.
Then when you know better, do better."

— *Maya Angelou*

My heart fluttered a little as I hit the "place my order" button and purchased our first online marketing course on how to private label products on Amazon. Spending several thousand dollars on a marketing course felt sharply out of my comfort zone, as I had always been one to just figure out things on my own. But, then I realized that investing in my education would pay dividends later on. At least I hoped so. As it turned out, investing in this course became one of the best business decisions I have made so far.

If I had known that the purchase would lead me to the multi-million-dollar exit from our company in just over 2 years, I would have had a lot more confidence and likely would have invested more. Instead, I found myself wondering, "Is this worth it?" and "Will we ever make our money back?" as I'm sure everyone in my position does at first. Once again, let me back it up to what led to our decision to purchase this online marketing course.

In the months prior, David and I had stumbled across several YouTube videos that boasted about the incredible successes that people were having from selling products on Amazon. com. The concept made sense: develop a desirable product, get it manufactured, send it to Amazon, and market it better than any other major brand or seller. It sounds difficult and complicated, but it's truly not. We already had the basics, and there was a lot of free information out there. Still, I kept wondering whether we were missing something. So, we ended up purchasing the more expensive online marketing course, and we simply counted that as another investment in our education. That decision was a turning point for me.

I learned that I could never go wrong by investing in information, knowledge, and/ or education. Between the online courses, the books, and the podcasts, I was constantly immersing myself in the latest news and the best educational resources on eCommerce. It's a habit I still have today. If there is a course out there on a business or marketing, I find the time and resources to take it.

In fact, when I started my first business as a freelance graphic designer, I read a book creatively titled, "How to Become a Freelance Graphic Designer." I already knew a lot about graphic design, but I knew very little about striking out on my own as an independent freelancer. The author carefully laid out the steps I needed to take if I wanted to achieve my goal of "freelance freedom."' I devoured that book. I even wrote in the margins. I went so far as to dog-ear my favorite pages. Essentially, I become a student again - to learn my way out of my less-than-desirable living situation. Put simply: I invested in myself so that I could invest in my company, and thus, my company ended up investing in me.

MAKING THE INVESTMENT

Every breakthrough, every great business advance I've made, has come from, or been supported by, an interest in continuing my education. I know that when I stop learning, I stop growing. Being a mom, I had to organize my time more efficiently than ever before. Being able to invest in my education became more of a challenge, but it was a challenge that I readily accepted. I know, and I want my kids to know, how important it is to continue learning even as an adult with a college education. Learning certainly does not stop there.

Knowledge is a critical component to success. Become an insatiable learner and you will be amazed by how much you can accomplish. While I had a wonderful college experience that helped me get a job, it was the entrepreneurial education that I received by independently investing in my after-college knowledge that catapulted me to a level success I never dreamed possible.

To pull it all off, I had to get creative and stay motivated. Here are the three steps that worked best for me:

STEP ONE: *Find a topic or business venture you're curious about.*

Search for as much free information or content as you can find. Start on Google and YouTube, but don't stop there. Podcasts, free webinars, and e-books are a plenty on the internet today. These are great places to start when you are feeling out a new idea. Consume only the FREE content in the beginning. This step is simple but necessary, so take notes. Basically, it allows you to make a better investment both in your education and in your ability to evaluate of all the information and sources discovered.

STEP TWO: *Settle on a course or book that you feel like would take your business or idea to the next level.*

Evaluate the costs. A book is an easy purchase. An online course is a larger investment so make sure you take your time evaluating their reputation. One good place to start is to jump on some Facebook groups in your area of interests. There may be someone there who has taken the course or has heard whether it's a good value.

STEP THREE: *Make a way to make the investment.*

If business training is something you are passionate about, or if you believe you can make a radical change in your life, find a door to opportunity by making the investment in yourself. One idea is to split the cost of a training course with a supportive and equally interested friend/partner.

INVEST IN YOURSELF

The bottom-line is: gaining knowledge is not something you will ever regret. Investing in your education means you are investing in yourself and what you can offer the world. Maybe it's your desire to have something of your own, or perhaps you are moving toward a powerful vision for your future. Either way, training, knowledge, and educating yourself is the only way you are going to get there. We are in the perfect time for that; this is the information age, for goodness sakes!

At the end of this book, I will provide a list of my favorite books and resources and I'll describe what I took away from each one. I'll also include my go-to online resources for education. I'll give a summary of each book and additional resource as well.

Write down five books or courses you feel would boost your business or idea to the next level. What tools for success can you get your hands on that would change your life or the life of your business?

Keep in mind that simply writing down this list of mental goodies is not quite enough. I think it's critical to set a deadline to pay for and complete each item. You can use the mini spreadsheet below to write out your list.

BOOK OR COURSE: COMPLETE BY:

1. _____   _____

2. _____   _____

3. _____   _____

4. _____   _____

5. _____   _____

An investment in knowledge pays the best interest.

- BENJAMIN FRANKLIN

DELAGATE THE MUNDANE

CHAPTER FIVE

"You can do anything, but not everything."

– David Allen

It was nearly midnight on a Tuesday night as I sat at my computer, hacking away at the keyboard to answer customer service inquiries from our Amazon clientele. It was late, I was bleary eyed, the time for bed had long since passed. I knew I should be sleeping, and yet I was sitting there diligently answering technical questions about how our zinc oxide powder was used for making sunscreen. Up until that point, I figured no one knew our product line better than us, so I made it my duty to serve each customer personally. After all, no one could answer the questions as well as I could. But, the reason I did that was not because I was some technical genius. It was because I had not educated anyone else on our line of products.

I had fallen into the trap that many entrepreneurs face when starting a new business: I believed that, for our business to be successful, I had to do it all on my own and that no one could do it better. I also believed hiring help or outsourcing, would be extremely expensive. I wanted to do everything and therefore keep a firm grasp over all the operations of our business. I got a sense of pride from being able to manage all aspects of the business with my own two hands (Who isn't proud to say they are a 'multi-tasking momma'?). But, what I eventually came to realize was that the business had a bottle neck and my name was written all over it.

Running all aspects of the business fell well within my scope of skills. For me to focus on working towards my vision for the company, however, and to continue designing my products, I had to let go of control of various parts of the business. This became especially apparent in the customer service realm. I believed (and still believe) that my customers deserve the direct attention that I simply cannot provide (unless I'm willing to give up my sanity). That's especially true when still trying to manage everything else. Some business owners mistakenly assume that hiring help is expensive or difficult. Fortunately, at least in this day and age, that is just not the case.

One of my favorite books, which I have referenced several times, is titled, "The Four Hour Work Week" by Tim Ferriss. Reading his book inspired me to outsource many of my duties to virtual assistants. By leveraging virtual assistants, I addressed my need to let go of the customer service aspect of our business. For this to happen, I broke it down into two digestible chunks:

1. MAKE THE MISSION CLEAR.

I put together an easy-to-read customer service manual for my assistants – one that was broken down to include:

✓ An introduction that explained the tone with which we should talk to customers

✓ Our general refund policy

✓ Our privacy statements

✓ A FAQ section for each our products

2. FIND THE HELP.

I created a job description on a website called Upwork.com. Freelancers from all over the world go there to find online jobs with business owners and individuals like me – well informed people looking for talented virtual assistants. Once, I posted a job on that website and found a fantastic India-based customer service rep for just $5 per hour. I passed along my training manual and continued monitoring her work to provide feedback along the way.

*NOTE: Individual results may vary.

That big, fat, scary task of hiring someone to take over an aspect of our business suddenly seemed effortless. It turned out to be much more expensive for me to personally provide the customer service for our company than to pay someone else to do. Hiring a virtual assistant for just $5 an hour truly paid off, and she even does a better job than me.

I have continued to outsource our social media marketing, google advertising, and website development needs. Each time, I can flex my delegating muscles as my workload becomes lighter and the company grows exponentially - all because I am more focused on my vision. I keep my eye on the prize and my attention stays centered on my greatest talents (instead of painstakingly answering mundane customer service emails at midnight on a Tuesday).

GETTING OUT OF YOUR OWN WAY

Don't get in the way of your business. Let it flourish organically under your direct yet subtle management. Hire others to do the tasks for:

✓ The things you don't enjoy doing

✓ The things you're not good at

✓ The things that take up most of your time

✓ The things that could be handled while you address more important matters

By hiring reliable and cost-effective help, you give yourself an extra set of hands when you need them the most. Thus, you feel less stressed out, and you might actually be able to focus on your calling for a change.

For me, the following method has always worked best:

1. DEFINE

What kind of control are you comfortable letting go of? Jot down 3-5 areas in your life that could benefit from outsourced help. Is it someone who can engage with your followers on Instagram or Twitter? Maybe you need a ghostwriter to post blogs for you. Get creative to define your needs.

2. CHOOSE

Pick one of those tasks and write down a quick job description. When I get stuck on what to include in my explanation, I sometimes search the jobs on Upwork to find a job description like mine to rewrite.

3. DELEGATE

Set a small budget for the project and test out an outsourced virtual assistant to handle one of the defined tasks for you. Be sure to check in after a couple of days to review progress and adjust if needed.

YOU CAN'T GO AT IT ALONE

You are the one with the vision—so you need to be working toward that vision and not answering every customer service inquiry or hand-labeling every single product! In the beginning, I did start by doing those things myself and I learned a lot. I learned what our customers where happy with or complaining about, and I learned exactly how long it took us to label each product so when we used a co-packaging company to do our labeling, I knew whether they were charging too much.

So, while it's always a good idea to get to know your business in the beginning by doing a lot of the work by yourself, you can't truly grow your company until you get out your own way and begin letting others do what they are good at. That's the best way to finally do what you are great at.

Great things in business are never done by one person. They are done by a team of people.

- STEVE JOBS

FIND YOUR PURPOSE & MEET YOUR PASSION

CHAPTER SIX

"You can fail at what you don't want,
so you might as well take a chance on
doing what you love."

– Jim Carey

....

Passion is a funny and fickle concept. Many people say, "Find your passion and do what you love." I won't lie and say that I don't love the businesses I've worked on because I truly do, but for me it's never been the business I'm passionate about. For me, it's always been about the purpose behind the business.

I stumbled upon this realization when David and I started our first company together—a photo booth rental business. We saw a huge opportunity to capitalize on a booming trend in weddings and it wasn't a huge investment. The concept was simple: for 3-4 hours at a time, customers rent our photo booth, which spits out a strip of four photos after each group photo session. We take care of the set up and tear down while customers experience the fun. What's interesting about our first business is not what we did to serve our customers. What's interesting is why we started the business in the first place.

David and I were newly married and, like many other couples, we were busy combining our individual debts. We had just finished a class on living a debt free life and realized that, with our fixed incomes, it was going to be a long, long road to achieve that goal. One day I pitched the idea to David about doing a photo booth rental company. In fact, I presented him with a business plan that I had written a year earlier but never acted on. He quickly recognized it as a great opportunity and a way to solve our problem of needing extra income. And so, we set out to create a successful company with one goal in mind: to pay off all of our debt.

I didn't believe this company was going to change the world or redefine our lives, it wasn't our life's passion. What we did was create a company to solve a temporary problem not just for customer, but to solve a problem that existed in our personal lives - the problem of debt. It was hard work and many weekends were spent with us being on our feet for hours, but after only 2 years we were nearly debt free. That experience taught us quite a few important lessons.

One lesson was that we never wanted to run a service-based business again. Running a service-based business took us from being employed by another company to being self-employed. It never really gave us the "freedom of time" we were looking for. The most important lesson we learned: to evaluate each opportunity against a set of criteria around our ideal lifestyle.

For starters, here are the top 5 questions that I use as a filter with every business idea I consider:

1. **HOW MUCH TIME OF MINE WILL THIS BUSINESS CONSUME?**
   Or more succinctly put, will it take over my life?

2. **CAN IT BE EASILY OUTSOURCED?**

3. **HOW DIFFICULT WILL IT BE TO MANAGE EMPLOYEES?**

4. **DOES IT HAVE LEVERAGE?**
   One of the aspects of a product based business I love is the power of leverage. By partnering with manufacturing facilities, products can be scaled quickly, efficiently, and without my hand touching each one. Compare that with hiring full-time employees or freelancing hours-for-dollars, and you can quickly see the attraction.

5. DOES IT ALLOW US TO HAVE FLEXIBILITY, SO WE CAN SPEND AS MUCH TIME WITH OUR KIDS AS WE WANT?

Yet another question I often ask myself when I am percolating business ideas: it a good fit for my skill set? Take our line of baby products for example. This was a perfect fit for me as a mom and as a designer. I could easily recognize trends and translate those into designs moms would love. I was a mom, I had lots of friends that were moms, and so I felt like I had intimate understanding of the demographic. However, if you asked mc how to launch a line of cell phone accessories and technical gadgets, I would have no idea where to begin. Therefore, not only is skill set an important factor to consider, but it also helps to identify with the audience that you are creating a product for. To summarize, invest time in what you know!

I bring all this about in a way to explain that while it's great to have a business that you feel you are passionate about, it's always important to identify a business that's fits your goals for your personal life as well. Passion is a huge word and it may seem daunting that you find a business that you have sustainable passion for. But building a business that is fun and exciting and helps you provide for your family while giving you more freedom? Now that's an idea that anyone can get passionate about!

✍ CHAPTER CHALLENGE

So, what business ideas do you have? What criteria are you looking for? Imagine your business with the end in mind.

What does it look like 3 years from now? Perhaps you are a running a team of super stars at a hip office in the downtown of your city. Or maybe you like working nights and mornings during naptime (like I did) while you have a team of virtual employees handling all the mundane, operational tasks. Do you see yourself collaborating or delegating?

You can use my filter questions below. Please feel free to add a few of your own as well!

1. **HOW MUCH TIME WILL THIS BUSINESS TAKE TO RUN A DAY/WEEK/MONTH?**

2. **CAN IT BE EASILY OUTSOURCED?**

3. **HOW DIFFICULT WILL IT BE TO MANAGE EMPLOYEES?**

4. **CAN I GROW AND SCALE THIS BUSINESS QUICKLY?**

5. **DOES THIS ALLOW ME TO SPEND TIME WITH MY FAMILY AND FRIENDS? (OR WILL I BECOME A WORKAHOLIC?)**

6. **WILL THIS BUSINESS BE PROFITABLE ENOUGH TO SUPPORT THE LIFESTYLE I DREAMED OF?**

DEVELOP YOUR GRIT

CHAPTER SEVEN

"With ordinary talent and extraordinary perseverance, all things are possible."
– *Thomas Fowell Buxton*

The doorbell rang. Why is it that the doorbell always rings when you are in the middle of changing a dirty diaper? I struggled with my son's diaper and hoped it was just a delivery man alerting me to a package at my doorstep. Then, the doorbell rang again. I ran downstairs, baby in arms, and opened the door to find the Fed Ex man waiting with a certified envelope for me to sign. I had an instant feeling I knew what he was holding, another cease and desist letter. I was right.

We had previously discovered that one of our products was infringing on a patent from another manufacturer. The company had sent us several cease-and-desist notices, and we were unknowingly in violation of the patent. So, we were doing our best to sell through our inventory to recoup some of the costs. What did this mean for us as a company?

Well, for one it meant that we were losing a product that brought in a significant source of revenue each month. It also meant that we had to liquidate inventory as quickly as possible, even if it was at a loss. It was a total bummer to say the least.

How did this affect us? Did we through our hands in the air and close up shop? Did we lose sleep over the official letterhead "From the Law Offices of...," and wonder why we ever started this company? No! While it was a challenge to recover the monthly revenue, an obstacle like this never diverted us from the goal of the company's success. It was yet another lesson in perseverance.

I have news for you, successful entrepreneurs run into obstacles quite often and it's less fun than a root canal. But, as you continue to flex the problem solving muscle, guess what? It gets stronger and obstacles no longer seem as daunting as you originally thought. This was definitely the case for me.

For the first two years of our small business, the obstacles seemed huge. Especially when financially we felt like there was a lot on the line. However, after overcoming one challenge after another, I came to expect bad news and each time the panic lessened.

Use the following tips and tricks to teach yourself how to overcome challenges and flex your perseverance muscle:

1. **DON'T MAKE THE PROBLEM TOO BIG.**
   Many times, we make problems much bigger than they need to be. It's easy to make something a huge deal and get emotional. Try to sleep on the problem, take a fresh set of eyes to it in the morning. Try to say to yourself, "Okay, I am going to take all emotion away and just look at this from a boring logistics standpoint." For the story I told above, it was as simple as losing several thousand dollars a month in revenue, so the solution needed to be replacing that product with another one that produced the same amount of revenue.

2. **REVIEW YOUR VISION.**
   Go back and read your vision statement. Remember why you are doing this business

in the first place, and remind yourself of what the ultimate goal is. When you reaffirm your desire to achieve your goal, you will see this problem for what it really is: another chapter along the way in your story to success.

3. GET SUPPORT.

Seek out positive, like-minded people. For us, we used a Facebook community of people who also sold physical products online to share our challenges with. Maybe it's a supportive spouse or friend, or maybe you're like me and you tell your 6 month old baby about your problems while he just spits and giggles in response (which helps me to realize how small the problem really is in the scheme of things).

4. KEEP TAKING ACTION!

Don't become paralyzed by fear of collapse and never quit taking action because you think it's never going to work. Take a small action towards solving your problem each day and you will be able to chip away at the issue in small steps. Just don't freeze up and do nothing!

5. EMBRACE THE UPS AND DOWNS OF LIFE.

Life is not all sunshine and rainbows; it's not even supposed to be. We all face challenges and deal with failure on a daily basis, but by embracing the idea that things won't always be perfect or go as planned, we can prevent the overly-emotional reaction towards our problems before they arise. With each challenge you overcome, you will become increasingly more comfortable when facing whatever comes your way next.

While the challenges are great, so are the opportunities.

- BILL FORD

When I look back on this amazing journey I have been on as an entrepreneur I am still amazed at how we got here. Starting out our little company by filling seaweed jars and then several years later, running a company that generated several million dollars a year in revenue. All this while working at home in my sweats, chasing around a toddler, and giving birth to a sweet little boy.

I often wonder what made me and my husband different from everyone else? What's the secret sauce that tipped us over into an overnight success? Part of the answer is the opportunity we had in front of us when we launched our own brand of physical products on Amazon. But literally, thousands of other people had the same opportunity, took the same courses and 90% never did anything with it. Why? I think it's the combination of all the lessons learned that took us from nothing to where we are today.

Of course, I had an ace card in my pocket because I am married to an amazing, brilliant, hardworking man. My kids are healthy, my family and friends are supportive, but without my partner in life I would not have achieved anything anywhere near the level of success that we were able to accomplish together. That is not to say that someone can't do it alone, don't get me wrong. I grew up watching my single mom work hard and achieve her dreams as well.

I hope that, in reading this book, you are inspired to go out and start a business and/or grow your existing one to the next level. I hope you can see that it is possible to be a mom, work from home, spend plenty of time with your kids, and still be an incredibly successful entrepreneur!

You can find me at www.momlifeinc.com for more ideas, inspiration and support!

Here is the list I promised, which includes my go-to online resources. I found each source essential to our success in the world of eCommerce.

AMAZING.COM

This website is truly deserving of its name. It is a one-stop e-learning shop for the online entrepreneur. Amazing.com is where we took the course that laid out systematic instructions on how to develop, sell, and market products on Amazon.com. This is the authority on the subject.

FREEDOM FAST LANE PODCAST WITH RYAN MORAN

This is terrific podcast for all Amazon entrepreneurs (and beyond). Full of inspiring interviews and insights, Ryan's podcast makes it easy for anyone to follow in our footsteps. I highly recommend it.

UPWORK.COM

This is a fantastic online resource for finding and hiring virtual freelancers and assistants. All transactions are secured through the website, and each freelancer has a rating and reviews. This is my go-to website for outsourcing. I use it for a wide variety of business and personal tasks— from managing a Facebook page to setting up a new Shopify website.

FIVERR.COM

This website is great for everything from getting 3D rendering of your product to having someone write a ghost blog post for your website. Every service starts at just $5, with optional add-ons and customizations available. I've had logo animations created and have even found people who can do video reviews.

TED.COM

If you've made any kind of foray into the world of learning and entrepreneurship, then you've most likely heard of TED.com. There are hundreds of TED talks ranging in topics from cutting edge science to what makes us happy. Here are my top 4 favorite TED talks that inspired me to look inward and take my success to the next level:

1. "Lean In" – Sheryl Sandberg

2. "Start with Why" – Simon Sinek

3. "Grit" – Angela Lee Duckworth

4. "The Surprising Science of Happiness" – Daniel Gilbert

MY RECOMMENDED READS

The following are a few of my favorite books and the insights I gleaned from each:

"The Seven Habits of Highly Effective People" *by Steven Covey*
This book was one of the first personal development books I read in college. It is a must-read, especially for the aspiring entrepreneur. The biggest takeaway I got from the book was learning how to be a "proactive person" versus being a "reactive person."

"Think and Grow Rich" *by Napoleon Hill*
I've read or listened to this book at least 3 times. Although it was originally published in 1937, all the concepts contained within it still ring true for me today. The big lesson I learned from this book was how powerful the human mind is, and how our conscious and subconscious thoughts can manifest our reality into something either positive or negative.

"Everyday Life Bible" *by Joyce Meyer*

There are so many powerful verses in the Bible that apply to my personal and professional life. If I had to choose just one, I'd say my favorite is the verse I used to begin this book: Habakkuk 2:2, "Write the vision, make it plain." This shows that having a vision is a timeless and effective necessity. Personally, I find it can be difficult to digest those old-school verses, so I rely on a study bible to help navigate the stories. The "Everyday Life Bible" by Joyce Meyer does a fantastic job of making the stories of the bible relatable and the advice actionable.

"The Four-Hour Workweek" *by Tim Ferriss*

To say I loved this book would be an understatement. Ferris does such an amazing job of challenging the long-held concepts about what it means to be rich and what a balanced life should look like. Reading this book was one of the biggest inspirations for us to start a product-based online business.

"Rich Dad, Poor Dad" *by Robert Kiyosaki*
This is another book that bucked at the status quo, challenging what it meant to live a wealthy lifestyle. Reading this book provided a necessary paradigm shift, providing priceless insights on how to manage money and what it looks like to be a successful business owner.

"On Becoming Baby Wise: Giving Your Infant the Gift of Nighttime Sleep" *by Robert Bucknam M.D. and Gary Ezzo*
Let's face it, without baby's naptime and those glorious hours of sleep at night, we would never get much accomplished. I am so thankful that I was recommended the book Babywise when I was pregnant with my first child. It is an essential guide to creating healthy sleep habits during the first year of your babies' lives. Both of my kids are great sleepers as a result!

YOU CAN FIND ME AT **WWW.MOMLIFEINC.COM**
FOR MORE IDEAS, INSPIRATION AND SUPPORT!

69050016R00068